This Journal Belongs To:

*A new commandment
I give unto you, That
ye love one another;
as I have loved you,
that ye also love one
another.*

John 13:34

Date:

Today I am Grateful For:

_____

_____

_____

_____

_____

_____

_____

_____

_____

_____

_____

_____

_____

Yea, though I walk through the valley of the shadow of death, I will fear no evil: for thou art with me; thy rod and thy staff they comfort me.

Psalms 23:4

Date:

Today I am Grateful For:

_____

_____

_____

_____

_____

_____

_____

_____

_____

_____

_____

_____

_____

Train up a child in the way he should go: and when he is old, he will not depart from it.

Proverbs 22:6

Date:

Today I am Grateful For:

_____

_____

_____

_____

_____

_____

_____

_____

_____

_____

_____

_____

*Let not your heart
be troubled: ye
believe in God,
believe also in me.
John 14:1*

Date:

Today I am Grateful For:

_____

_____

_____

_____

_____

_____

_____

_____

_____

_____

_____

_____

_____

_____

Humble yourselves in the sight of the Lord, and he shall lift you up.

James 4:10

Date:

Today I am Grateful For:

_____
_____
_____
_____
_____
_____
_____
_____
_____
_____
_____
_____
_____
_____
_____

Therefore all things whatsoever ye would that men should do to you, do ye even so to them: for this is the law and the prophets.

Mathew 7:12

Date:

Today I am Grateful For:

_____

_____

_____

_____

_____

_____

_____

_____

_____

_____

_____

_____

_____

_____

_____

_____

Therefore if any man be in Christ, he is a new creature: old things are passed away; behold, all things are become new.
2 Corinthians 5:17

Date:

Today I am Grateful For:

_____

_____

_____

_____

_____

_____

_____

_____

_____

_____

_____

_____

Watch ye and pray, lest ye enter into temptation. The spirit truly is ready, but the flesh is weak.

Mark 14:38

Date:

Today I am Grateful For:

...The LORD is my light and my salvation; whom shall I fear? the LORD is the strength of my life; of whom shall I be afraid?

Psalm 27:1

Date:

Today I am Grateful For:

_____
_____
_____
_____
_____
_____
_____
_____
_____
_____
_____
_____
_____

For the Son of man is come to save that which was lost.

          Mathew 18:11

Date:

Today I am Grateful For:

_____
_____
_____
_____
_____
_____
_____
_____
_____
_____
_____
_____
_____

Nor height, nor depth, nor any other creature, shall be able to separate us from the love of God, which is in Christ Jesus our Lord.

Romans 8:39

Date:

Today I am Grateful For:

Cast thy burden upon the LORD, and he shall sustain thee: he shall never suffer the righteous to be moved.
Psalms 55:22

Date:

Today I am Grateful For:

_____

_____

_____

_____

_____

_____

_____

_____

_____

_____

_____

_____

_____

_____

_____

Giving thanks always for all things unto God and the Father in the name of our Lord Jesus Christ
        Ephesians 5:20

Date:

Today I am Grateful For:

_____

_____

_____

_____

_____

_____

_____

_____

_____

_____

_____

_____

_____

The fear of the LORD is the beginning of knowledge: but fools despise wisdom and instruction

Proverbs 1:7

Date:

Today I am Grateful For:

_____

_____

_____

_____

_____

_____

_____

_____

_____

_____

_____

_____

Enter into his gates with thanksgiving, and into his courts with praise: be thankful unto him, and bless his name

Psalms 100:4

Date:

Today I am Grateful For:

Pray without ceasing.

1 Thessalonians 5:17

Date:

Today I am Grateful For:

_____

_____

_____

_____

_____

_____

_____

_____

_____

_____

_____

_____

_____

For the LORD is good; his mercy is everlasting; and his truth endureth to all generations.
Psalms 100:5

Date:

Today I am Grateful For:

_____

_____

_____

_____

_____

_____

_____

_____

_____

_____

_____

_____

_____

For I the LORD thy God will hold thy right hand, saying unto thee, Fear not; I will help thee.

Isaiah 41:13

Date:

Today I am Grateful For:

_____

_____

_____

_____

_____

_____

_____

_____

_____

_____

_____

_____

_____

Thy word is a lamp unto my feet, and a light unto my path.
Psalms 119:105

Date:

Today I am Grateful For:

_____

_____

_____

_____

_____

_____

_____

_____

_____

_____

_____

_____

_____

And this is the confidence that we have in him, that, if we ask any thing according to his will, he heareth us:

1 John 5:14

Date:

Today I am Grateful For:

_____

_____

_____

_____

_____

_____

_____

_____

_____

_____

_____

_____

_____

Beloved, let us love one another: for love is of God; and every one that loveth is born of God, and knoweth God.
                    1 John 4:7

Date:

Today I am Grateful For:

_____

_____

_____

_____

_____

_____

_____

_____

_____

_____

_____

_____

_____

_____

...The earth is the LORD'S, and the fulness thereof; the world, and they that dwell therein.
Psalms 24:1

Date:

Today I am Grateful For:

_____

_____

_____

_____

_____

_____

_____

_____

_____

_____

_____

_____

_____

_____

A man's heart deviseth his way: but the LORD directeth his steps
                    Proverbs 16:9

Date:

Today I am Grateful For:

_____
_____
_____
_____
_____
_____
_____
_____
_____
_____
_____
_____
_____
_____

And all things, whatsoever
ye shall ask in prayer,
believing, ye shall receive.
Mathew 21:22

Date:

Today I am Grateful For:

_____

_____

_____

_____

_____

_____

_____

_____

_____

_____

_____

_____

_____

And call upon me in the day of trouble: I will deliver thee, and thou shalt glorify me.
Psalms 50:15

Date:

Today I am Grateful For:

And God saw every thing that he had made, and, behold, it was very good...
Genesis 1:31

Date:

Today I am Grateful For:

_____

_____

_____

_____

_____

_____

_____

_____

_____

_____

_____

_____

_____

And he said unto them, Go ye into all the world, and preach the gospel to every creature.
Mark 16:15

Date:

Today I am Grateful For:

_____

_____

_____

_____

_____

_____

_____

_____

_____

_____

_____

_____

And thou shalt love the LORD thy God with all thine heart, and with all thy soul, and with all thy might.
                                 Deuteronomy 5:5

Date:

Today I am Grateful For:

And he said, The things which are impossible with men are possible with God.
Luke 18:27

Date:

Today I am Grateful For:

_____

_____

_____

_____

_____

_____

_____

_____

_____

_____

_____

_____

And he saith unto them,
Follow me, and I will make
you fishers of men.
Mathew 4:19

Date:

Today I am Grateful For:

_____

_____

_____

_____

_____

_____

_____

_____

_____

_____

_____

_____

_____

Be of good courage, and he shall strengthen your heart, all ye that hope in the LORD.
Psalms 31:24

Date:

Today I am Grateful For:

And I say unto you, Ask, and it shall be given you; seek, and ye shall find; knock, and it shall be opened unto you.
Luke 11:9

Date:

Today I am Grateful For:

_____

_____

_____

_____

_____

_____

_____

_____

_____

_____

_____

_____

_____

And if I go and prepare a place for you, I will come again, and receive you unto myself; that where I am, there ye may be also.

John 14:3

Date:

Today I am Grateful For:

And it shall come to pass, that whosoever shall call on the name of the Lord shall be saved.

Acts 2:21

Date:

Today I am Grateful For:

_____

_____

_____

_____

_____

_____

_____

_____

_____

_____

_____

_____

And Jesus said unto them, I am the bread of life: he that cometh to me shall never hunger; and he that believeth on me shall never thirst.

John 6:35

Date:

Today I am Grateful For:

_____

_____

_____

_____

_____

_____

_____

_____

_____

_____

_____

_____

But the meek shall inherit the earth; and shall delight themselves in the abundance of peace.

Psalms 37:11

Date:

Today I am Grateful For:

Call unto me, and I will answer thee, and show thee great and mighty things, which thou knowest not.
Jeremiah 33:3

Date:

Today I am Grateful For:

_____

_____

_____

_____

_____

_____

_____

_____

_____

_____

_____

Commit thy way unto the LORD; trust also in him; and he shall bring it to pass.
Psalms 37:5

Date:

Today I am Grateful For:

_____

_____

_____

_____

_____

_____

_____

_____

_____

_____

_____

_____

_____

Create in me a clean heart, O God; and renew a right spirit within me.

Psalms 51:10

Date:

Today I am Grateful For:

*And ye shall know the truth,
and the truth shall make you
free.*

John 8:32

Date:

Today I am Grateful For:

_____

_____

_____

_____

_____

_____

_____

_____

_____

_____

_____

Every word of God is pure: he is a shield unto them that put their trust in him.
Proverbs 30:5

Date:

Today I am Grateful For:

_____

_____

_____

_____

_____

_____

_____

_____

_____

_____

_____

_____

_____

_____

Favour is deceitful, and beauty is vain: but a woman that feareth the LORD, she shall be praised.
Proverbs 31:30

Date:

Today I am Grateful For:

_____
_____
_____
_____
_____
_____
_____
_____
_____
_____
_____
_____
_____

For thou art my rock and my fortress; therefore for thy name's sake lead me, and guide me.

Psalms 31:3

Date:

Today I am Grateful For:

_____
_____
_____
_____
_____
_____
_____
_____
_____
_____
_____
_____

Be not forgetful to entertain strangers: for thereby some have entertained angels unawares.
        Hebrews 13:2

Date:

Today I am Grateful For:

_____

_____

_____

_____

_____

_____

_____

_____

_____

_____

_____

_____

God is my strength and power: and he maketh my way perfect.
2 Samuel 22:33

Date:

Today I am Grateful For:

_____

_____

_____

_____

_____

_____

_____

_____

_____

_____

_____

Behold, I stand at the door, and knock: if any man hear my voice, and open the door, I will come in to him, and will sup with him, and he with me.

Revelation 3:20

Date:

Today I am Grateful For:

_____

_____

_____

_____

_____

_____

_____

_____

_____

_____

_____

_____

Bless them that curse you,
and pray for them which
despitefully use you.
Luke 6:28

Date:

Today I am Grateful For:

*Blessed are the peacemakers:
for they shall be called the
children of God.*
                    Mathew 5:9

Date:

Today I am Grateful For:

_____

_____

_____

_____

_____

_____

_____

_____

_____

_____

_____

_____

Blessed are they which do hunger and thirst after righteousness: for they shall be filled.
Mathew 5:6

Date:

Today I am Grateful For:

_____
_____
_____
_____
_____
_____
_____
_____
_____
_____
_____
_____

Many are the afflictions of the righteous: but the LORD delivereth him out of them all.
Psalms 34:19

Date:

Today I am Grateful For:

_____

_____

_____

_____

_____

_____

_____

_____

_____

_____

_____

_____

65416848R00058

Made in the USA
Lexington, KY
11 July 2017